THE VIKINGS

First published in the UK in 2019 by

Ivy Kids

An imprint of The Quarto Group

The Old Brewery

6 Blundell Street

London N7 9BH

United Kingdom

www.QuartoKnows.com

British Library Cataloguing-in-Publication Data
A catalogue record for this book is available from the British Library.

ISBN: 978-1-78240-904-5

This book was conceived, designed & produced by

Ivy Kids

58 West Street, Brighton BN1 2RA, United Kingdom

PUBLISHER Susan Kelly

MANAGING EDITOR Susie Behar

ART DIRECTOR Hanri van Wyk

DESIGNER Kevin Knight

IN-HOUSE DESIGNER Kate Haynes

IN-HOUSE EDITORS Lucy Menzies &
Hannah Dove

Manufactured in Guangdong, China TT052019

1 3 5 7 9 10 8 6 4 2

My FIRST
Fact File

THE VIKINGS

EVERYTHING you NEED to KNOW

BY PHILIP STEELE   ILLUSTRATED BY STEF MURPHY
CONSULTANT: DR RAGNHILD LJOSLAND

IVY KIDS

CONTENTS

EVERYTHING you NEED to KNOW

INTRODUCTION

About 1,200 years ago, villagers in Western Europe were scared. They heard terrible tales about armed warriors from the northern lands of Scandinavia.

These Northmen, or Vikings, came in their ships, sailing along coasts and rivers. They attacked villages and towns with axes and swords. They burned down churches and carried off all the gold and silver they could steal. They even captured people and carried them off as slaves. Many Vikings had frightening names, such as 'Blooodaxe' or 'Skullsplitter'.

The Vikings sailed far and wide, exploring and settling in new lands. They invaded large parts of the British Isles, Ireland and France. They sailed on to Iceland, Greenland and the mainland of North America. They sailed south to the sunny Mediterranean Sea. They traded far from home in snowy Russia and in the markets of Baghdad in Iraq.

The Vikings were not just warriors, though. They were farmers, fishermen, blacksmiths and shipbuilders. They were skilful woodworkers and weavers, jewellers, poets and storytellers. Their assemblies, where laws were agreed, would later become parliaments and law courts.

Archaeologists today have found Viking treasure, ships and buildings. These show how Viking men, women and children really lived long ago. They prove that the Vikings were far more than just mean fighters. They were amazing adventurers who shaped the world as we know it today.

In this book, you will see the terms 'CE' and 'BCE'. 'CE' means 'Common Era', or during the age of Christianity. 'BCE' means 'Before the Common Era', or before Christianity.

The Vikings were incredible sailors who explored far and wide in their longships.

WHO WERE THE VIKINGS?

'Vikings' is the name we give to people who lived in Scandinavia in Northern Europe, between 1,200 and 900 years ago. They became known as adventurous sailors and great warriors who travelled in their longships to find new lands. At home, they were farmers, fishermen and craftspeople.

The Vikings raided (attacked) people in Europe in order to take control of their land.

The Vikings wrote words using letters called runes. They didn't use a pen and paper, but carved the runes into rocks or wood.

Some Vikings fished, while others farmed for food.

The Vikings used Scandinavia's lakes and coastline for fishing, and forests for fuel.

SCANDINAVIA

Most Vikings lived in southern Scandinavia where it was warmer.

Vikings cut wood for fires to keep them warm in the snowy winters.

CRACK THE CODE

The Viking alphabet is called the 'futhark', which is the sound of its first six runes. Only 16 runes were used during Viking times.

ᚠᚢᚦᚭᚱᚴ ᚼᚾᛁᛆᛋ ᛏᛒᛘᛚᛦ
f u t h a r k h n i a s t b m l R

Can you translate these runes into modern English?

ᚦᛁᛋ ᚠᛁᚾᚭ ᛁᛋ ᚭ ᛋᚭᚱᚴ
ᚦᚭᛏ ᛁᛋ ᛁᛏᛋ ᚠᛁᛏ

_____

_____

See page 48 for the answer

QUICK FACTS

The word 'Vikingr' meant going on a voyage or raid. The word 'Vikingar' (Vikings) may have been given to the people who raided.

SOCIETY

Viking society was divided into different groups. At the top was the king. The first Viking kings controlled small regions. Over the years, kings became more powerful and ruled over whole countries. Viking noblemen, called 'jarls', came next. They were rich and powerful owners of large areas of land, horses and ships. Most Vikings were called 'karls'. Some were wealthy and owned land and houses, while others were poor. Warriors, seafarers and settlers were karls. At the bottom were 'thralls': slaves who had no rights and were forced to work very hard as labourers or servants.

QUICK FACTS

The Vikings had a strong sense of honour and they could be easily upset. Quarrels could turn into fights that lasted for years.

Women ran the farms and homes while the men were away fighting. They were in charge of the household budget and carried the keys to buildings and stores. They were skilled spinners and weavers.

LAW AND ORDER

Arguments and disputes were sorted out at a public assembly known as the 'Thing'. Men would gather from all over the region and a 'lawspeaker' would tell them about the law. A thief might have to pay back money to his victims, a criminal could be exiled to a foreign land, and some disputes were sorted by combat between two people.

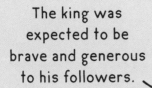

The king was expected to be brave and generous to his followers.

Jarls were powerful chieftains, with many warriors.

Karls owned land and traded. Most karls were farmers.

Thralls were slaves, who had to work very hard for their masters.

THE LONGSHIP

Many Vikings lived on coasts and islands, or beside rivers. Ships were often the quickest way to travel. People in Scandinavia had been building boats for a thousand years or more, and the Vikings were the best sailors in Europe. The sea was their route to fame and fortune, and enabled them to raid and settle in unknown lands. It was the longship that gave them their fearsome reputation as sailors and raiders.

The helmsman steered the ship using his broad steering oar as a kind of rudder.

Oars could be as long as 8 metres.

A longship was powered by sail or oars. The crew needed to be ready for storms, rough seas or enemy attacks.

There was one big sail, woven from wool.

The carved dragon prow was designed to scare the enemy or evil spirits.

Longships were up to 17 metres long and held up to 80 men.

DESIGN A LONGSHIP PROW

You need:
Card
Scissors
A felt-tip pen
An adult helper

The Vikings were great woodcarvers, and they liked to decorate their best ships. Sometimes the prow of a longship was carved in the shape of a beast, a snake or a dragon. Its snarling jaws may have been intended to terrify the enemy or drive away evil spirits, or just impress other Vikings! You can design your own scary beast for a prow. Draw an outline on light card and cut it out. Draw in the detail.

QUICK FACTS

A longship sailed at speeds of about 9 to 19 kilometres per hour, with a top speed of perhaps 28 kilometres per hour.

AT SEA

Life at sea was hard. Longships were open boats, with no cabins. A large cloth could be put up to shelter the rowers. This could be taken ashore, along with tents, to set up a camp. Viking crews had no proper maps. They followed coastlines, looking out for familiar features such as headlands. They also looked at the positions of the Sun and stars. Spotting certain birds meant that land was close. A wind vane on the mast showed which way the wind was blowing, and helped them to navigate.

QUICK FACTS

There was no 'inside' on a Viking ship. Weapons, clothes and food would be kept dry in the crew's sea chests.

MAKE A WIND VANE

You need: Stiff cardboard, scissors, a ruler, gold acrylic paint, a paintbrush, a felt-tip pen, sticky tape, a wooden stick, an adult helper

1. Draw a right angle on the cardboard, with the horizontal line measuring 10 centimetres and the vertical line measuring 6 centimetres.
2. Draw a curved shape from one line end to the other. Cut it out and paint it gold. With a felt-tip pen, draw on snakes, lions, dragons or birds.
3. Tape the short side to a stick and push it loosely into the ground. Watch the wind blow it around!

Oarsmen put up with sea spray, icy winds and burning hot sun.

The sailors had to survive on food that would last on a long voyage, such as dried or salted meat and fish, apples, nuts and cheese. Fresh fish could be caught on the way.

TRADING

Viking merchants sailed around Northern Europe and as far south as Asia, selling and buying goods. They sailed in ships called 'knarrs', which were wide and deep with room for cargo. Traders sailed or rowed up rivers, too. These trading expeditions were set up by karls. Most Vikings who went could farm, row, sail or fight as well as haggle for the best deal.

EUROPE

ASIA

Scandinavia and Russia were centres of the fur trade.

Germany provided swords of the finest quailty.

Silks and spices were imported from Asia.

QUICK FACTS

The Vikings traded locally as well as in distant lands. They exchanged goods such as amber, wine and tin, or paid with silver bars or coins.

MINT SOME MONEY

Goods were bartered (exchanged) with other items.

Vikings sold fish, and falcons for hunting.

You need:

Silver card

Scissors

A thin-tipped black marker pen

An adult helper

By the 900s CE, Viking kings began to make coins. Imagine you are a Viking king. You want to design and mint (make) some coins to show how powerful you are. The design might show a ship, an axe or a sword. Cut out some coin-sized discs from silver card, and draw on your designs with the marker pen.

RAIDING AND SETTLING

The Vikings used their fast longships to attack villages and towns along coasts and rivers in Europe. Villagers barely had time to race home from the fields before armed warriors were swarming ashore. As well as taking food and treasure, Vikings looked for better farmland and new lands to settle in. Once they won, they would build new towns and villages and bring new families to these new lands. The best items to steal were those that were easy to carry: gold, silver, weapons, tools, clothes, furs and jewellery.

Vikings often attacked Christian monasteries. The monks had chests of coins and valuables.

Buildings were burnt down and villagers were seized as slaves.

Ships would bring whole families and households to create new settlements.

NORSE DETECTIVE

Vikings left traces of their language, Old Norse, in the names of islands, bays, towns and buildings across many parts of the world. Here are some examples. Can you use a map to find any more?

-ey or -ay = island
e.g. Bardsey (Wales), Olney (USA)

-thwaite = meadow
e.g. Le Thuit (France)

-ness = headland
e.g. Inverness (Scotland)

-by = settlement or farm
e.g. Whitby (England), Grimsby (Canada)

-vik = bay
e.g. Hoyvik (Faroe Islands),
Reykjavik (Iceland)

-kirk = church
e.g. Ormskirk (England),
Falkirk (Scotland)

QUICK FACTS

At first, Viking raids mostly took place in summer, when sailing was easier. However as the raiders grew bolder, they began to spend winters overseas as well.

WARRIORS AND ARMOUR

Viking warriors were mostly karls, who were called away from farming to go to war. Only a few were full-time, paid soldiers. Viking warriors might march to battle, sail there in ships or ride on horseback. Most of the fighting was on foot. Many Vikings battled in their everyday clothes. The richest warriors might own a byrnie (a shirt of metal mail). This was made of small, interconnected iron rings.

Most iron helmets were round or shaped like a cone, and padded inside.

Sword blades were about 70 to 80 centimetres long.

A small axe weighed about 800 grams.

Spears were 2 to 3 metres long.

The best helmets had bars to protect the nose, eyes and cheeks.

Shields were up to 1 metre wide and weighed 5 to 7 kilograms.

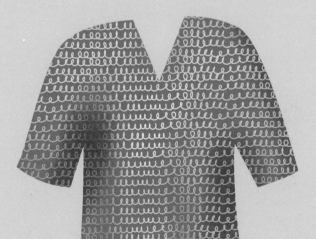

A mail shirt weighed about 12 kilograms. It came down to the thigh.

MAKE A SHIELD

You need:

Heavy cardboard

Scissors

Sticky tape

Coloured paints

A paintbrush

An adult helper

Viking shields were often painted in bright colours and bold patterns. Make a shield to fit your size by cutting out a large circle from heavy cardboard. Tape a cardboard handle on the back. On the front, paint a grey circle in the centre and add a coloured pattern around it, perhaps with swirls, quarters, stripes or a cross.

QUICK FACTS

In an age before guns, warriors fought closely, person to person. Viking warriors were known as fiendish fighters and writers wrote down exciting stories about them, called sagas.

ATTACK!

By the 840s CE, small groups of Viking raiders were joining up to fight in larger forces, perhaps numbering a thousand or more. These armies might be led by a king. Viking armies were able to march inland and fight their enemies. Walls, ditches and fences were often built around towns to protect them from being attacked. Combat was exhausting. The fighters had to leap, kick, lunge and punch. All the time they were looking for an unguarded spot they could attack.

QUICK FACTS

Viking armies had enough warriors and weapons to attack or besiege cities such as London, Paris, Ghent and Hamburg.

Wooden towers were set on fire with flaming arrows.

FLY THE RAVEN BANNER

You need:

Fabric

Scissors

Fabric paints

A paintbrush

A bamboo cane

An adult helper

Some Viking armies flew a small battle flag with a picture of a raven. This bird was an emblem of the great god Odin, the lord of battle and death. To make a flag, cut out a triangle shape from the fabric, with a curved lower edge. Make small cuts into the curved edge to create a fringe. Use fabric paints to draw the raven. Attach your battle flag to a bamboo cane.

A catapult hurled boulders to knock down the city walls.

A battering ram could smash down the city gates.

CLOTHES

Viking clothes for men and women were colourful. Viking women and girls generally wore a long shift of linen, with a shorter dress or pinafore made of wool over it, held by shoulder straps and fastened by brooches. Men and boys wore a tunic of linen under an outer tunic of wool, often trimmed with fancy braid. Trousers could be baggy or narrow. There were hooded cloaks, caps of wool and fur hats.

QUICK FACTS

Spinning, weaving and sewing were carried out by women in the home. Textiles were woven on a large, upright loom.

Wealthy Viking women would wear jewellery.

Brooch to fasten shoulder straps

Hair pin

MAKE A BROOCH

You need: Stiff card, scissors, paint, paintbrush, sticky tape, safety pin, an adult helper

A very wealthy Viking woman would wear the very best brooches to show just how rich she was. Two oval brooches of bronze decorated the shoulder straps, while smaller brooches fastened cloaks and shawls. You can cut out brooch shapes from stiff card and paint with Viking animal designs from the Internet. Tape a safety pin to the back and wear with pride!

Married women wore their hair in a bun, under a headscarf.

Linen shift

Woollen dress

Headscarf

Fur hat

Woollen tunic

Linen tunic

Woollen trousers

Men wore their hair long, and were expected to have a beard and moustache.

Leather shoes, boots or slippers were often worn with woollen socks.

Children wore the same sort of clothing as their parents, just in smaller sizes.

FARMING

Most Vikings lived by farming the land. In warmer areas where the soil was good, the farms were quite near to each other, sometimes forming villages. In colder regions with poor soil for growing crops, there were fewer farms. Viking farmers grew rye, barley and oats. In warmer regions, they could plant wheat. Hay was grown to feed the animals. Cattle grazed on fresh grass in the summer.

QUICK FACTS

Farms were home to land-owning families, free labourers and slaves. Around the longhouse, where the family lived, there might be a wash house, barns, cowsheds, a dairy and a smithy (a blacksmith's workshop).

WHAT'S IT FOR?

All these tools might be found on a Viking farm. What do you think they were used for?

See page 48 for the answers

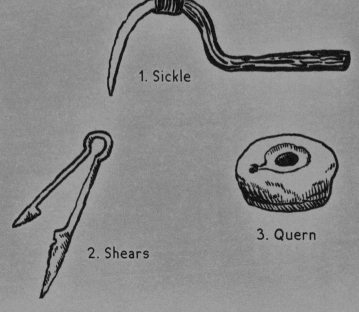

1. Sickle

2. Shears

3. Quern

Throughout the year, most Vikings spent their time looking after their animals and crops on farms.

In spring, farmers planted seeds of rye, barley and oats.

In summer, the sheep were sheared to provide wool for clothing.

In autumn, the crops were harvested.

In the cold days of winter, cattle were kept indoors and fed on hay.

THE LONGHOUSE

At the centre of the farm stood the longhouse, perhaps 30 to even 60 metres long, and 5 to 7 metres wide. It was usually built from wood. The roof was thatched (made with straw) or tiled with wood. In areas where wood was hard to find, such as Iceland, the longhouse might be stone-built, with a roof of turf (grass and mud). As time passed, extra rooms might be added at the sides.

QUICK FACTS

A longhouse needed to be big to fit in a family, their relatives or guests and farm workers. One end was sometimes also used to house farm animals in winter.

Mattresses were filled with straw or feathers.

Chests, baskets, barrels, buckets and hooks were used for storage.

TOWNS

Viking towns often started as ports and grew larger from about 800 CE. Inside the town, the streets were paved with lengths of heavy timber, which acted as pathways. Houses were thatched and similar inside to a longhouse. A few towns survived past the Viking age, and became the big cities we know today.

Walls were made of wattle (criss-crossed sticks), which were plastered with daub (mud or straw mix) in between strong wooden posts.

The roof was covered with straw or mud.

Cauldrons were made of iron and hung on chains over the fire.

Weaving area

Peat, brushwood or logs were burnt in the firepit.

The centre of family life was the hearth. This was a firepit, which provided heating, light and cooking. Smoke escaped through holes in the roof.

29

FOOD AND FEASTS

Family meals were taken mid-morning and in the evening. Oats, barley or rye were used to make porridge or a coarse bread, which could be baked on an iron or stone griddle. Cheese was made from the milk of sheep, goats and cows. Hunting brought in hare, deer, elk, boar and wild birds, and useful plant foods such as nettles, berries and nuts. The eggs of seabirds were collected from cliffs. Leeks, onions, turnips, cabbages and peas were grown in the fields. Herrings were a big part of the diet, and meat such as beef, pork, mutton, goat and chicken was also eaten.

QUICK FACTS

Chiefs liked to entertain guests and enjoyed feasting and drinking. A seasonal festival or a family celebration could last for days. Ordinary Vikings would eat a simpler diet of bread, stewed vegetables and some meat and fish.

VIKING SNACK

You need: A bowl, a spoon, oats, an apple, blueberries, hazelnuts, milk, honey

We don't have any Viking recipes as such, but we do know which foods they ate. Your mission is to prepare some healthy food for a hungry friend! In a bowl, mix up some oats, apple slices, blueberries, hazelnuts, milk and honey. On the side you could provide a wholemeal bun with some goats' cheese.

Honeycomb

Wooden cup

Barley bread

Meat was usually boiled or stewed.

Fruit

Cheese

Eggs

Herring and vegetables were often eaten.

Soapstone dishes

Honey was used to sweeten meals.

Porridge

Wooden plate

GROWING UP

You'd need to be lucky to grow up at all in Viking times. Many children died as infants from incurable diseases. Childbirth was a cause for celebration. Nine days after the birth, the father placed the baby on his knee and sprinkled the head with water. He or she was given a name and recognized as a member of the family. Guests brought gifts to the ceremony. However, before long, children were expected to work hard and help with all the chores that the adults had to do.

Toddlers played with dolls, toy animals or balls made of felt.

Young children fought with toy swords to prepare for real fights.

Young children were expected to help their mothers with chores such as milking cows.

QUICK FACTS

Viking children had to grow up quickly and learn skills such as swimming, farm work and sword fighting. They would need these skills when they were grown-up.

Girls got married once they reached their early teens.

By the age of 15, boys were old enough to fight alongside men.

MAKE A BOUNCY FELT BALL

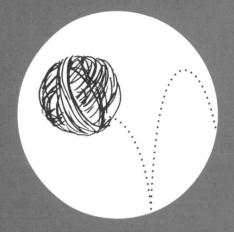

You need:

Some wool strands

A bowl

Washing-up liquid

Water

A tablespoon

A cup

An adult helper

1. Mix 4 tablespoons of washing-up liquid with 6 cups of warm water in a bowl.

2. Screw up a small ball of woollen fibre with your hand, then wind strands around it. When your ball is twice as big as the one you want, dip it in the water. Keep rolling it between the palms of your hands for 10 minutes, without squeezing.

3. When it has shrunk, rinse it under a cold tap and let it dry. Tie some coloured woollen yarn around it and let it bounce!

FUN AND GAMES

Men played sports such as wrestling, tug-of-war, weight-lifting, skating and swimming. There were bat-and-ball games, too. Most sports were played to the extreme and often ended in violence. Board games were always very popular. Viking families played dice, chess, draughts and games similar to backgammon. One game was called 'hnefatafl'. Players had to protect their king while he tried to escape to his corner castles. The Vikings loved words, especially riddles, rhymes and poems. Travelling poets called 'skalds' would attend the feast of a jarl or a king and compose verse to music.

QUICK FACTS

Viking poets liked to use kennings — phrases that described something without directly saying what it was. The listener had to work out the meaning. So, the wind could be called a 'tree breaker' and the sun a 'sky candle'.

Scandinavian music of the early Middle Ages was not written down. It remains a mystery.

Tales of magic and heroic adventures were told around the fire.

These Viking chess pieces were carved from walrus ivory in the 1100s CE.

MUSIC

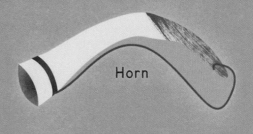

Horn

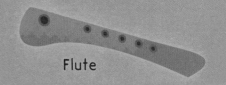

Flute

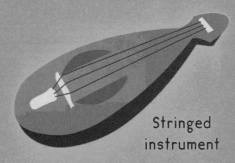

Stringed instrument

Little is known about how the Vikings danced or played music, but we do know that they played pipes and flutes made from bone or horn, and stringed instruments including a harp. Ibrahim al-Tartushi, a traveller from Spain, visited Hedeby in 965 CE. He said that Viking songs sounded like dogs or wild animals howling!

Wrestling was a popular sport but it could get violent.

ARTS AND CRAFTS

In the days before factories, it was individual craft workers who made the things that people used, bought or sold every day. In a Viking town there might be carpenters, carvers, blacksmiths, tanners of leather, shoemakers and glassmakers. Woodturners used lathes to shape wooden bowls and poles. At home, potters made jugs, pots, loom weights and oil lamps. Carved wood decorated houses, furniture, ships, wagons and, later, churches. Favourite Viking patterns included knots and loops, birds and fish, beasts and dragons.

This carved animal head was found in Norway.

Silversmiths from Jutland made this brooch.

BRIGHT COLOURS

Viking textiles and tapestries were brightly coloured with dyes made from plants. The leaves of the woad plant turned cloth blue. The husks of walnuts produced a brown colour. The root of a plant called madder made things red. The flowers of weld, or dyer's rocket, gave a yellow dye, while heather stems were used for dark green.

Skilled blacksmiths could turn
metal into useful objects.

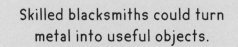

2. Bellows
make the
fire really
hot, so that
the iron
becomes
softer.

1. First the iron is heated
and then hammered flat.

3. The hot, soft
iron is hammered
into shape.

4. The item is
cooled off in a
bucket of water.

QUICK FACTS

Viking jewellers
used gold, silver and
glass beads to make
rings, necklaces
and bracelets.

Blacksmiths made essential
items such as swords,
nails and keys.

GODS AND GODDESSES

The Vikings believed there was a human world (Midgard) and a home of the gods (Asgard) connected by a shimmering rainbow bridge, called Bifrost. There were nine such worlds inhabited by humans and all sorts of other beings, such as gods, elves, dwarfs, giants and dragons. This universe was held together by the roots of a gigantic ash tree called Yggdrasil. These old myths and legends survived even after Christianity came to the Viking lands in the 800s CE.

The cats Bygul and Trjegul pulled Freyja's chariot.

Freyr (left) and Freyja (above) were the god and goddess of fertility and love.

Loki was the mischief maker.

Thor was the god of thunder. His hammer Mjollnir was forged by dwarfs.

CHIEF OF THE GODS

Odin had two ravens, Hugin and Munin.

Odin was chief of the gods.

The chief of the gods was called Odin. He had only one eye and rode across the stormy sky on his eight-legged horse Sleipnir. He owned two wolves called Geri and Freki. His two ravens, Hugin and Munin, flew around the world to bring him news. Odin lived in a great hall called Valhalla. Warriors who died bravely in battle were taken there to feast with the gods.

Odin had two wolves, Geri and Freki.

QUICK FACTS

According to some Norse myths, there were originally two tribes of gods and goddesses. The two tribes fought each other before they joined together.

CUSTOMS AND FESTIVALS

The Vikings' belief in spirits, gods and goddesses was rooted in everyday life. The goddess Frigg ruled over weddings and marriage. That was why Vikings got married on Frigg's Day, or Friday. It was also thought that the fate of humans was decided at birth, by female beings called 'Norns'. It is thought the Vikings celebrated May Day and Midsummer's Day. In Sweden, people continue the May Day tradition by lighting bonfires to welcome the return of light.

In the winter, Vikings decorated their houses with evergreen plants.

THE COMING OF CHRISTIANITY

For many years pagan and Christian beliefs existed side by side in the Viking lands. Some new Christians still prayed to Thor in an emergency. In 960 CE, the Danish King Harald Bluetooth became a Christian. During the 1000s CE, Christianity spread through the Viking lands, but some people resisted and still made sacrifices to the old gods.

In midsummer, Vikings may have made bonfires to celebrate the solstice (the longest day of the year).

In autumn, animal sacrifice, known as a blot, took place to please the gods.

QUICK FACTS

The Vikings held festivals throughout the year to honour their spirits, gods and goddesses.

FUNERALS

Death was never far away in the Viking period. Disease, warfare and giving birth meant that many people died young. Men and women who survived into their fifties were thought of as old. Funerals varied greatly between regions and from one period to the next. Some Vikings were cremated on open fires or pyres after they died. Most were buried in the earth, in simple graves or under a mound.

Rich Vikings were buried with everything they might need in their next life.

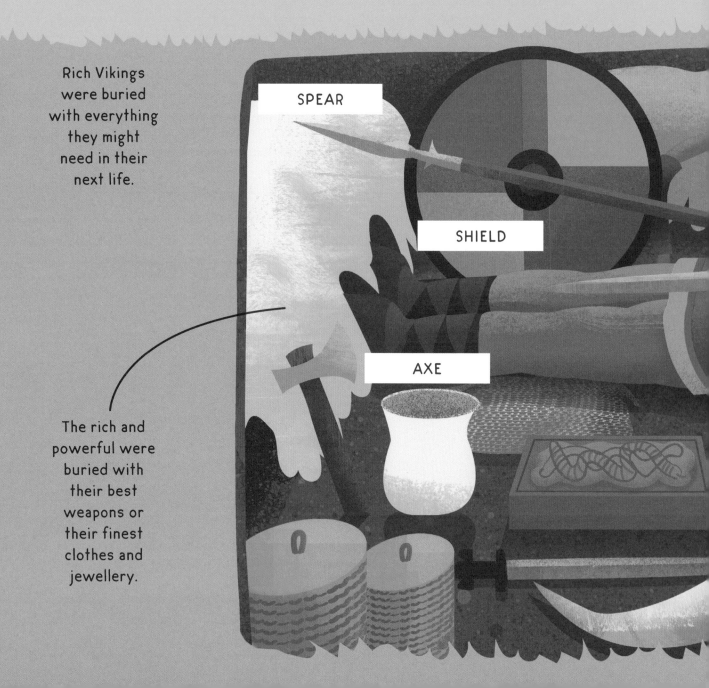

SPEAR

SHIELD

AXE

The rich and powerful were buried with their best weapons or their finest clothes and jewellery.

Sometimes, stones were placed around the grave in the shape of a ship.

BOW

FOOD

GHOST SHIP

A beautiful ship was excavated by archaeologists in Norway over 100 years ago. It had lain buried under a mound of earth since the year 843 CE. It was made of oak and decorated with carvings. Inside were the skeletons of two women, one in a very fine dress and linen veil. Also in the ship were richly carved sleighs and a wagon, a bed post, textiles and tapestries.

QUICK FACTS

Kings and queens were sometimes buried in finely carved wagons with their best horses, or in beautiful longships. These may have been seen as transport to other worlds.

EXPLORATION

Although their largest area of settlement was across central and northern England, the Vikings were great travellers and settlers. Hoards of Viking treasure are still being discovered today. One hoard found in Norway in 1834 had items from France, Russia, England, the Byzantine empire and the Middle East. They even reached parts of North America, where they encountered Native American tribes.

Newfoundland in North America, Greenland and Iceland.

Western Europe
Middle East
Russia

Areas of Viking Exploration

In North America, the Vikings fought with the Native American tribes but also exchanged goods with them.

EASTERN LANDS

The Vikings sailed across the Baltic Sea and travelled into Russia. Here they traded in amber, silver, fur, honey and slaves. Some Vikings travelled to Baghdad (the capital of modern-day Iraq), and went on to create trading routes all the way to China.

QUICK FACTS

The Vikings overran large areas of Britain and Ireland and attacked the mainland and islands of Western Europe. They travelled west to the Faroe Islands, Iceland, Greenland, Labrador and Newfoundland, and east to the Middle East.

END OF THE VIKING AGE

During the 1000s CE, Europe was going through many changes. Small kingdoms and territories were uniting under powerful kings. The Vikings were becoming Christian. Danes, Norwegians and Swedes went on to play an important part in European history, but many Viking settlements overseas became swallowed up by new kingdoms such as England, France or Scotland. However, the Viking way of life still has an influence on our modern lives.

Traditional Viking boatbuilding skills are still used to make a boat called a skiff.

Up Helly Aa, a festival held in Shetland, a Scottish island, celebrates Viking traditions by burning a Viking-style ship.

Many of the days
of the week are based
on Viking names.

Some modern parliamentary
traditions can be traced back
to the Viking assemblies.

QUICK FACTS

The Vikings left a rich legacy. This
included language, styles of art and
design, storytelling, boatbuilding,
assemblies and parliaments.

VIKING NAMES

Today, there are still people
whose surnames are based
on the Viking system. Vikings
identified babies as 'son of'
or 'daughter of' their father.
This is how it worked:

Eirik (= ever-powerful)
Thorvaldsson (= son of Thorvald)
'the Red'

Sigrid (= beautiful victory)
Tostadottir (= daughter of Tosti)
'the Proud'

Vikings loved giving people
nickames, too: often funny or rude
ones! Try giving yourself one, such
as James son-of-Tom 'the Nerd',
or Lily daughter-of-Steve
'the Blue Haired'.

GLOSSARY

BELLOWS A machine that creates a gust of air. It is used to start a fire.

BESEIGE To surround and cut off the enemy, so that they cannot receive supplies or get help.

BYZANTINE EMPIRE The eastern part of the Roman Empire.

CARGO Goods carried on a vehicle.

CHIEFTAIN A Viking leader of a tribe.

EXILE A punishment in which a person is sent away from where they live and cannot return.

HELMSMAN A person who steers a boat.

LATHES A machine that turns a piece of wood, metal or glass so that it can be worked on.

MIDDLE AGES A period of Europe's history that lasted from the 5th century to the 15th century.

PAGAN Someone who follows a pre-Christian or non-Christian faith.

PROW The projecting front part of a ship.

RUDDER An underwater blade that can be moved in order to steer a boat.

SCANDINAVIA The area of Northern Europe that includes Denmark, Norway and Sweden.

SETTLEMENT A place where people build an area to live.

SHIFT A woman's simple dress or an under-dress.

SOLSTICE When the Sun is at its greatest distance from the Equator – in summer, this is the longest day of the year and, in winter, it is the shortest.

TEXTILES A material made from natural or man-made fibres.

WIND VANE A flat piece of metal that moves to show the direction of the wind.

ANSWERS:

Page 9 Crack the Code
This fish is a shark
That is its fin

Page 26 What's it For?
1. Sickle – cutting corn
2. Shears – cutting
3. Quern – grinding grains